FRACTAL ANALOGY

A FRACTALLY ANALOGOUS UNIVERSE

AS ABOVE, SO BELOW

Fractal Analogy

Written by Nicolaas A Gad

Copyright © 2024 by Nicolaas A Gad

All rights reserved.

No part of this book may be reproduced, distributed, or transmitted in any form or by any means, including photocopying, recording, or other electronic or mechanical methods, without the prior written permission of the publisher, except in the case of brief quotations embodied in critical reviews and certain other non-commercial uses permitted by copyright law. For permission requests, write to the publisher.

Self-Published by

Nicolaas A Gad

Albertgad67@gmail.com

ISBN: 978-1-7637114-1-9

First Edition: September, 2024

Cover Design by Nicolaas A Gad

Printed in Australia

N. A. GAD

INDEX

PAGE
       INTROUCTION
1   ANALOGOUS DIMENSIONS
16   FRACTAL LIFE
29   THE HUMAN EXPERIENCE
58   FRACTAL FORCES
66   REVELATION

INTROUCTION

Inside the brain there are neurons, and when someone thinks of something, a certain combination of these neurons fires in a particular pattern. That combination of neurons isn't actually the thing the person is thinking of, it just represents or has the meaning of what the person is thinking of. These patterns require an observer to interpret them. If the observer is not the neural firing in the brain, then what is the observer? What is the interpreter?

Within the neural firings, there will be a certain neuron pattern that means tree, but it isn't actually a tree. And so when you are thinking of a tree, and can see that tree in your mind, where is that tree that you see? It isn't physically in the brain, as there is only a neuronal pattern that means tree. The tree can only be seen subjectively by the observer thinking of it. It is in an intangible place. It is in a non physical space.

How can one show evidence for this intangible place? It is impossible, however it doesn't discount its existence. The tree is in a place of ideas and thought. This place contains good and bad, subjective feelings and thoughts, and even the very existence of what we see, hear and experience, as what we see and experience is also the result of the interpretation of neural firings in the brain (albeit these signals are received from the senses, but nonetheless are experienced in the mind). This place contains all ideas, feelings and experiences. It contains what we know as qualia - the subjective experience of something.

And so we exist in this place of thought without knowing it, without realizing the fabric of reality isn't as separate or different from the fabric of dreams as one thought. We believe this reality is somehow more real and less magical than it is. More serious and less connected than it should be. More random and less meaningful than it tells us. Life is but a dream, and so life is what you make it.

And while life can be seen as one thing or another, with this dream comes a persistency of its nature. It does have a structure, it does have laws, and it does have a 'physical' aspect. And with this lies one of the fundamental dichotomies of the universe. The metaphysical and the physical. The observer and the observed. The tangible and the intangible. Even further at its core is perhaps the most fundamental dichotomy, something and nothing. And from this stems the two sides we see in everything. Left and right. Up and down. Dark, light. Day, night. Awake, asleep. Hot, cold. Good, bad. This apparently inherent binary nature of the universe requires exploration to understand why it seems to be so. It is just one feature that shows the universe seems to be structured in a particular way; and this way is a logical way - a way by where thought can make sense of it, and a way by where thought can create it.

1

ANALOGOUS DIMENSIONS

INWARD IS UPWARD

Understanding the relationship dimensions have to each other can help conceptualize higher dimensions.

HERE, WE HAVE A ZERO DIMENSIONAL (0D) *POINT*:

0D POINT

It has no space (length, width and height) and no time.

HERE, WE HAVE A ONE DIMENSIONAL (1D) *LINE*:

ITS ONE DIMENSION IS LENGTH

It consists of two 0D points defining its bound, but contains potentially infinite 0D points within it, and so can also be visualized as:

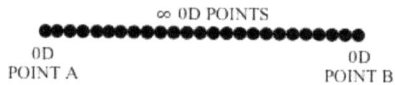

HERE WE HAVE A TWO DIMENSIONAL (2D) *SQUARE:*

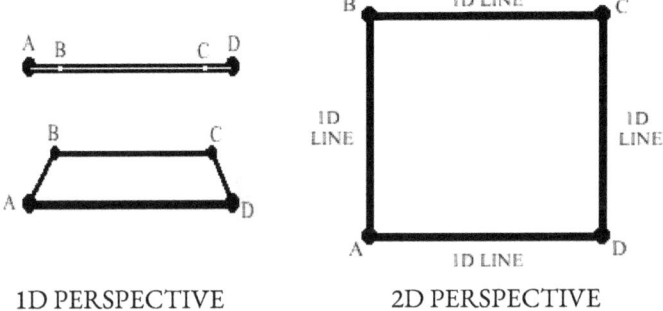

1D PERSPECTIVE   2D PERSPECTIVE

ITS TWO DIMENSIONS ARE LENGTH AND WIDTH

It consists of four 1D lines defining its bound, but contains potentially infinite 1D lines within it, and so can also be visualized as:

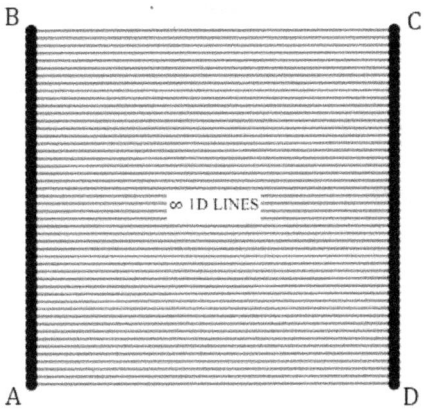

Note that the square isn't comprised of any 1D lines in particular, and diagonal lines from a to c, b to d, or any combination, can be an example of one 1D line out of the infinite lines comprising this shape. This will be important for understanding time

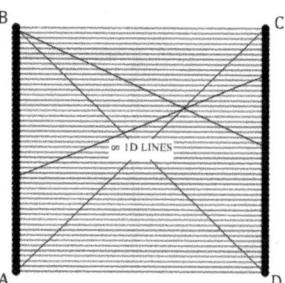

From the 1D perspective, a smaller line appears 'inward' from the larger one, with lines connecting the ends.

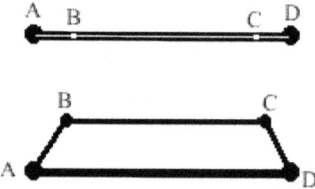

We can interpret that the smaller line is further away than the larger line, but perspective forces it to appear to us as smaller and 'inward'.

"PERSPECTIVE FORCES US TO PERCEIVE DISTANCE IN ADDITIONAL DIMENSIONS AS INWARD"

HERE WE HAVE A THREE DIMENSIONAL (3D) *CUBE*:

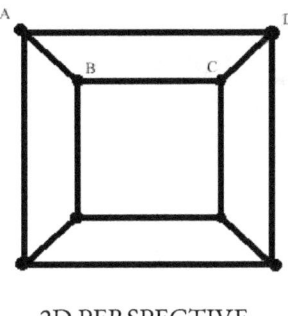 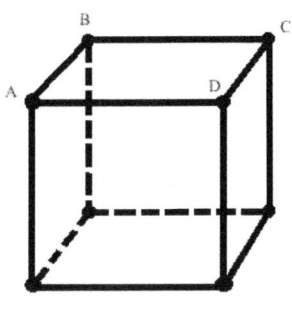

2D PERSPECTIVE   3D PERSPECTIVE

ITS THREE DIMENSIONS ARE LENGTH, WIDTH AND HEIGHT

It consists of six 2D squares defining its bound, but contains potentially infinite 2D squares within it, and so can also be visualized as:

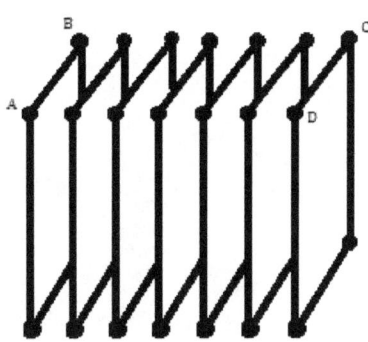

In the 2D perspective, a smaller square appears within the larger one, with lines connecting the corners:

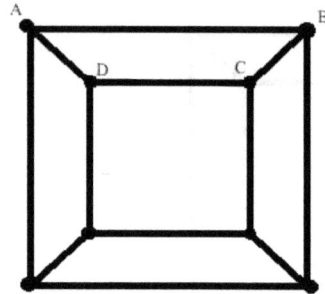

We can interpret that the inner square is further away in the third dimension than the larger square, but perspective forces it to appear to us as smaller and inward.

HERE, WE HAVE A FOUR DIMENSIONAL (4D) *HYPERCUBE*:

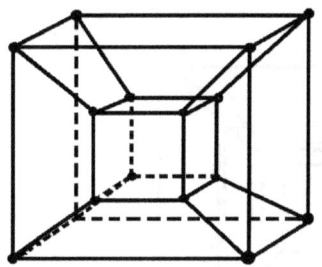
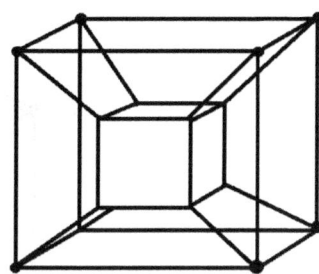

3D PERSPECTIVE

ITS FOUR DIMENSIONS ARE LENGTH, WIDTH, HEIGHT AND TIME

It consists of eight 3D cubes defining its bound, but contains potentially infinite 3D cubes within it, and so can also be visualized as:

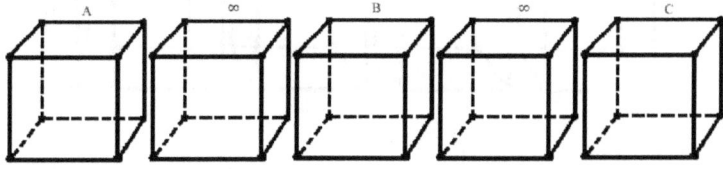

From the 3D perspective, a smaller cube appears within a larger one, with lines connecting the corners:

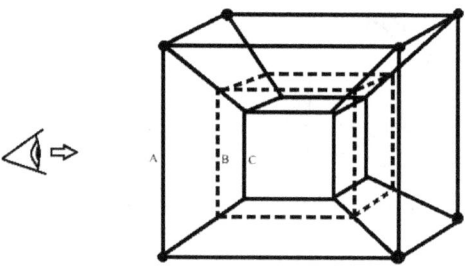

It can be interpreted that the inner cube is further away in the fourth dimension (time), but perspective forces it to appear to us as smaller and inward.

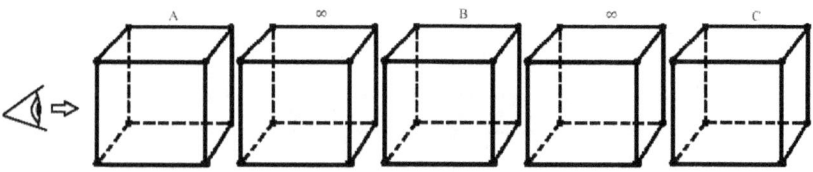

And so our perspective of looking at time from the third dimension may be responsible for the direction of time we perceive, and why from this perspective time flows in one direction for the observer and not the other (a to c and not c to a).

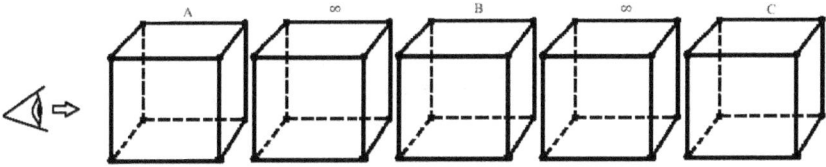

This shape or timeline only has a single outcome and path it can follow (a to c), and so is deterministic in nature.

This timeline can also be represented using dots (0D points) as placeholders for the different cubes (frames in time) which make up the timeline:

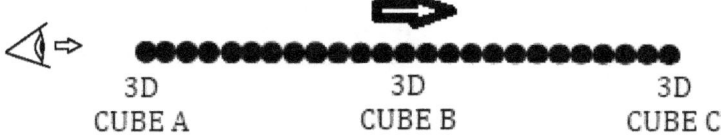

HERE WE HAVE A 5 DIMENSIONAL (5D) *5-CUBE*:

It consists of 10 4D hypercubes defining its bound, but contains potentially infinite 4D hypercubes within it. This can be represented as:

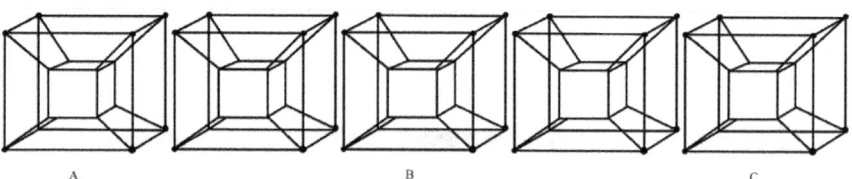

A   B   C

Between a and c are potentially infinite hypercubes.

Since each hypercube can be represented as a line (timeline), we can then represent this 5D 5-cube as:

Where each timeline consists of potentially infinite 3D cubes/frames in time.

Just as a 2D square isn't comprised of any 1D lines in particular, this 5D 5-cube isn't comprised of any 4D timelines in particular, and directions from any starting point to any outcome are possible.

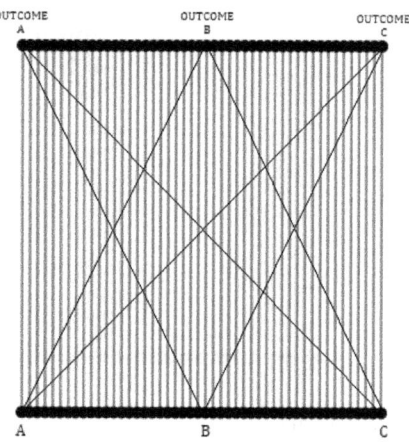

This allows for multiple outcomes to be possible, and so is not deterministic in nature and allows for free will.

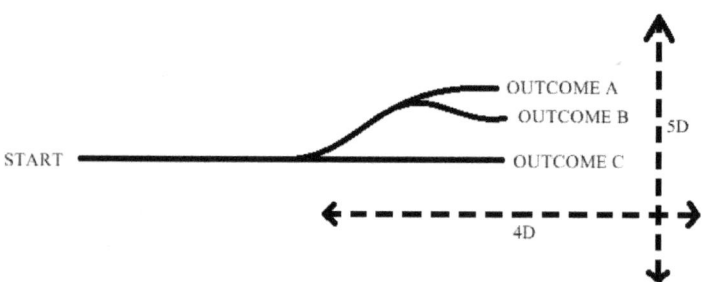

The analogies for the dimensions follow for up to three dimensions in time at least (totalling a minimum of six dimensions). Going above six dimensions can become convoluted and confusing as to where and what these dimensions would be. Some have suggested there is at least one more set of three dimensions, or possibly infinite, which lie outside of what is conceivably relevant to human existence.

The significance of the numbers 3, 6 and 9 has been referenced and noted by many individuals and belief systems in history, which may be a result of their correlation with each set of dimensions that are a fundamental structure of existence.

The three dimensions of time have sometimes been referred to as 'the time cube', though it may manifest as a time-sphere or any other shape. While five dimensions allows for all potentialities and possible outcomes to exist within our universe with its starting conditions (set laws of physics), stacking multiple 5D universes perpendicularly above each other gives a total of six dimensions, which allows for all potentialities within all timelines of every possible universe (with differing laws of physics to our own) to exist. This allows for the existence of universes and timelines with differing starting points and conditions to the one we live in, and encompasses everything that is fathomable to humans.

These dimensions reside within a containment of their own, which in the case of there being a total of six fathomable dimensions, is a seventh layer of existence that all things conceivable to human's resides in and stem from. This seventh layer is the most fundamental element to human existence, and is referred to by some as "the all", "the source", "the absolute", "God", and many other names. It is the conceivable absolute; a single and unified all encompassing existence and awareness. It is everything, and there is not anything that it is not. It is something that all things are a part of.

The seventh dimension is the conceivable containment of everything including consciousness, and is the conceivable all, however if dimensions truly extend beyond seven, outside of what is conceivable, then seven is not truly the all. In some religions, twelve is regarded as representing completeness, and seven may be only what humans can comprehend. The one true absolute source of everything is likely incomprehensible, and is only represented by what is comprehensible, however for what is comprehensible and for what is understandably relevant to this human experience, the seventh dimension is the all.

Seven is a number that surfaces frequently in belief systems and reality itself: the 7 chakras (Hinduism), which correspond to the 7 colors of the light spectrum (physics), the 7 factors of enlightenment (buddhism), the 7 heavens (Islam), and the 7 days of creation (Christianity/Judaism). These directly correlate to and represent the seven dimensional structure of the conceivable universe.

The dimensions can be interpreted as being analogous to the all encompassing and absolute (God) creating the universe in six days (dimensions), and rests (resides) on the seventh (dimension/day). In Islam these dimensions may be represented as the seven heavens, described as layers of existence that ascend one above the other, however in Islam allah's throne is not the seventh heaven (seventh dimension) but is above it. And so God isn't 'up in the sky', but is 'up in the dimensions', and as the seventh dimension, God is all encompassing and omnipresent, as God is everything, seen and unseen. While each belief system represents the dimensions differently, they all seem to describe the same structures.

2

FRACTAL LIFE

HIGHER DIMENSIONAL BEINGS

"It is an individual's duty to write into the universe their story. An individual's travel through time is an individual writing, the present moment being the point of contact between the pen and the page - marking each next letter. This should not be done carelessly, or without thought, as so many do. For those distracted and off course, now is the time to decide on that next letter, as there is only ever now to make the next mark."

As the universe and everything within it are present in many dimensions above what is normally perceived, humans too are present and extend into these higher dimensions.

It is often communicated to look inward to find one's higher self, and this should be more apparently true after understanding the perceived relationships between dimensions, and that 'inward is upward'.

Conceptualizing one's higher self, starting with the fourth dimension, one would expect to see each version of the human form from birth to death as one shape, fully observable as a whole.

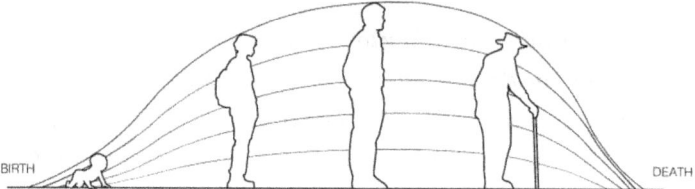

Similar to the visualization of a 4D hypercube as the infinite cubes (frames of time) it contains within it, when viewing the 4D human self, it can be observed as the infinite 3D versions of itself from birth to death (each frame in time from birth to death).

It is said that time speeds up as one ages - time seems to go by faster the older one gets. As one grows in space, objects seem smaller, and as one grows in time, periods of time seem smaller.

It is also mentioned that in death, one's whole life flashes before their eyes - an ascension through the dimensions toward a higher dimensional perspective of one's own whole self. This may be toward returning to the source, or toward existing as their whole higher dimensional selves. At the end of a day, we return home, and at the end of a life, we also return home.

To live a life may be to shape one's lower dimensional existence, and after death they may exist as their whole self, unbounded by any one moment of time. If one shapes a life of misery, worry and pain, it will eternally be so, and if one shapes a life of positivity and good, it will eternally be so. One's life remains how they shaped it while living.

This higher dimensional perspective of one's whole self allows the connection each human has to one another to be visually apparent. Our birth is connected to our mother and father; the origin of each shape is its parents:

From a 3D perspective it appears each human is separate and independent from one another, however, each is connected in the fourth dimension (time). This connection is only observable from a higher dimensional perspective.

The reality of this connection can be realized by using a lower dimensional analogy.

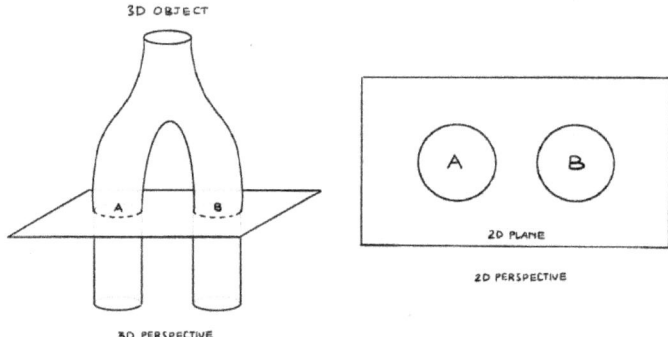

This 3D shape appears as two separate 2D shapes (a and b) from the perspective of the 2D plane intersecting it, however these 2D shapes are physically connected as one shape when observed from a higher dimensional perspective.

In this same way, the connections humans have with each other can be perceived when observed from a higher dimensional perspective. From this perspective, humans can be seen as one being, which is only seemingly separated in the 3D intersection of reality humans observe. Each human is a cell within a higher dimensional organism.

The connections humans have in higher dimensions may extend further from the fourth dimension to the fifth and sixth as well. These connections make up the human superorganism, which is a part of life as a whole. Each other species has similar connections that comprise a similar superorganism of their own kind. The human superorganisms connections to all other forms of life makes up the body of life as a whole (known as the tree of life), and this can be illustrated as the complete evolutionary tree.

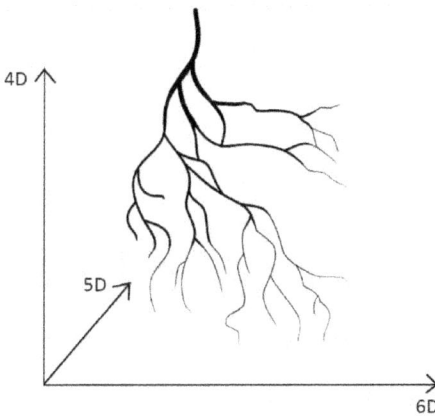

This six dimensional structure (tree of life) contains all paths and outcomes for all of life - every action and possibility of every possible organism within all paths evolution can take inside every possible universe.

Like leaves on a tree, or cells of a body, humans (and the human superorganism), and all living things humans observe in their reality, are part of this larger, more powerful and seemingly all encompassing higher dimensional organism (referred to as life), but are not life itself.

Life contains all living things. It is not the absolute, but a part of and creation of the absolute. It is an independent being, and as a higher dimensional being, it and any others like it experience and are present in what humans call the past, present and future, and all the potentialities of these, all at once.

While the all is the source of conscious awareness, and everything within it is a part of the all, life may be its instrument to interact with itself, learn and improve to develop itself - or, life may just be the universe's way of having an experience.

While life's true structure is imperceivable from the unaltered perspective of a human, some of its structures and processes can be observed.

THE BODY OF LIFE

"Us, and existence, was created in the image of God"

As the human body is made up of many individual cells organized in a way that allows for a larger organism to emerge and exist, humans too are cells that are each a part of a larger organism. Each human (and each organism found in nature for that matter) are only a small part of the higher dimensional body of life.

From the perspective of the human, the structure and cells of the superorganism humans are a part of seems disconnected and separated, unlike the cells that make up the human body, which are joined with an observable connection. Keep in mind though, when viewed from a higher dimensional perspective, the connection humans have to each other to form this larger organism becomes perceivably apparent.

The cells of humans and the humans of society are both organized and function in analogous ways, from the distribution of resources and the maintenance of homeostasis, to allowing for the emergence of higher intelligence.

The same structures appear at multiple levels, from a cell comprising of organelles, to a body comprising of organs, to society comprising of organizations. Analogous structures appear in cells, the body and society, and apply even higher when the human superorganism is seen as one organ in the body of life as a whole.

Roads correspond to the circulatory system of arteries, veins and capillaries, transporting nutrients to where they are needed. Humans correspond to cells, which organize into organs or organizations. Each cell/human serves a particular function to support the organ/organization they are a part of, and each organ/organization serves a particular function to support the body as a whole.

These analogous structures and their functions can become more apparent when laid out plainly:

1. Cells working together form into organs
2. Humans working together form into organizations.

Each cell/human serves a particular function to support the organ/organization they are a part of.

1. The *organs* of the human body all function together to serve the common goal of allowing the body to survive and thrive.
2. The *organizations* of society all function to serve a common goal of allowing society (the human superorganism) to survive and thrive.

1. When a cell *performs well* within the organ and body it is a part of, it is *rewarded* with the resources necessary for it to survive and thrive.
2. When a human *performs well* within the organization and society it is a part of, it is *rewarded* with the resources

(wealth, positivity, sustenance etc.) It needs to survive and thrive.

1. When a cell *does not perform* its function properly, it is excluded, terminated, or *negatively affected* in some way.

2. When a human *does not perform* its function properly, it is excluded, ostracized or *negatively affected* in some way.

Performing well is determined by how well a cell *serves its purpose,* which can become obvious when one follows their true path. This process is sometimes referred to as "karma", where good actions that help the body a cell is a part of is rewarded, and bad actions are punished.

The processes and systems of the body are often far too complicated for one of its cells to make a causal connection between their actions and what happens to them, and so synchronous events (synchronicities) and karmic reward/punishment are often regarded as 'coincidence', 'luck' or 'random chance'.

Noticing and paying attention to these 'coincidental' events that often feel unexplainable and in some way magical can give more clarity, meaning, purpose and fulfillment in life.

THE THINKING ORGANISM

"Everything is a part of consciousness, and so like humans 'have' consciousness, so does everything else, however, the conscious ant's ability to think is limited by the ant, much like the conscious rock's ability to think is limited by the rock; even if something is without thought, it is still a part of consciousness."

A higher dimensional organism is more capable and aware than its constituents.

A brain is made up of numerous nodes, each communicating messages between one another in complex patterns and networks that, as a whole, allow for more complex thought and behavior to emerge,

This is very similar to how the basic rules of communication ants follow and the messages they communicate between one another, as a whole, allow for more complex behaviour to emerge when they are looked at as a larger organism.

Like the nodes or neurones of the brain, humans too are a form of node, each communicating messages that travel in complex patterns and pathways throughout society. Messages and nodes self organize based on interest, popularity, relevance and necessity - one hears something from a friend, and they pass it on to their family, who passes it on to their friends.

Just like the complex patterns of communication between nodes in the brain allow for more complex thought and a larger and more capable awareness to emerge, so do the complex patterns of communication between humans, and so do the complex communication pathways of all of life.

Life is thinking, and the processes that allow for this can be observed as an idea or piece of information is passed along from one human to another, from social group to social group, culture to culture. It can be observed in the many individuals voting on decisions and ideas to decide as one. It can be observed in the ever going process of trying to reach a consensus among a population. These are the essential workings of the 'brain' of the larger superorganism called life - one that humans and all living organisms are a part of, and one that allows for more advanced thought and a larger awareness for consciousness to experience and use.

Life may sometimes be seen as God like in terms of its superiority and all encompassing presence throughout an individual's experience. It is however not *the* God, as in the creator or the all - it only resides within the all, and is limited in dimensional occupancy.

Life is limited to six dimensions, which includes all pathways of all evolutionary trees in all potential universes.

To solely acknowledge this being as *the* God is to worship only a part of and creation of the all, not the all itself.

As the all supersedes all that is fathomable, residing in or as the seventh dimension or beyond, the all and consciousness can only be defined by what it is not. It is not a single object, idea or being, and so is not anything in particular, but is everything as a whole.

3

THE HUMAN EXPERIENCE

DICHOTOMY

"There are two sides to every thing"

Upon first inspection, the universe appears to be dichotomous - meaning of two, or cut in two. There are two equal sides to the human form. There is left and right. Dark and light. Day, night. Male, female. Hot, cold. Young, old. Pain, pleasure. Positive, negative. Good and evil. God and devil. Something, nothing. The list has no limit, and the duality seems present in all things.

It is a universe split in two, mathematically represented as positive and negative numbers. A common question posed - how does something come from nothing? It is simply that something is the same as nothing, as a balanced universe comprising of positive and negative is equal to nothing (positive one plus negative one is equal to zero). Something and nothing are the same and may be seen as the first dichotomy, and from this all other dichotomies arise.

The dichotomous nature of the universe is represented by many cultures and religions. One of the most well known examples is God and the devil, which is just one representation of the dichotomy of positive and negative - what is good and what is not good. Yin and yang. The dark and the light.

And while light and dark may seem opposite, they are truly a measure of one thing: how light something is. There is no darkness, just an absence of light.

We see with most dichotomies that they are a result of one's perception from within what they are perceiving. A ruler with two ends is not two separate things; the ends are merely different points on the same ruler. The ruler is one, that when observed from the middle appears to have two distinct sides. This dichotomy is the result of an observer's separating perspective. If one labels one thing, they must label the other. Without left there is no right. There is no pain without pleasure. You can't have nothing without something; they are codependent.

Each dichotomy seems to be the two extreme representations of the same thing, and some may be simplified as the lack of something and abundance of something. Light and dark is a measure of the abundance of light. Hot and cold is a measure of the abundance of heat. When seen in this way there is no antilight, as darkness becomes an absence of light, and there is no negative heat, as coldness becomes the absence of heat. There is only zero light and some light, or zero heat and some heat.

Some dichotomies however cannot easily be described in the same way, and are more obviously dependant on the observer. Left and right is dependant on the observer, not independent of the observer. The dichotomy of the future and the past is also dependant on the observer. These examples more easily demonstrate that most dichotomies are the result of the observer being within what they are perceiving, and so most dichotomies are a matter of perspective. Whether something is hot or cold depends on where the observer is situated on the scale of hotness and coldness, and this applies to dichotomies like good and bad.

The fundamental core of these dichotomies is the observer and the observed. Awareness and the universe. Consciousness and its creation. The intangible and the tangible. This fundamentally may be cause of the separating perspective all individuals have.

And as an observer with this separating perspective, it is up to each individual to decide which end of each scale they wish to reside in - for good and bad, positive and negative, it is up to each individual to choose which side they wish to occupy and experience, and which side they wish to shape their existence towards, which can sometimes be more challenging than it seems.

As dichotomy manifests in everything one experiences, it gives rise to the reverse law of attraction; a paradox where as one tries to be or do something, they attract the opposite. When an individual chases something, it runs away. If one tries to be happy, they will never be happy. If one tries to be rich, they inherently are labeling themselves as not rich. One must not try to be what they want to be to become it. As alan watts has said, "when you are wanting something so badly, you grab onto it too hard and break it, and when it is not achieved or obtained, it feels as though something has been lost. You need to let go of wanting, and only then will you be satisfied with the present".

Just as an individual's timeline is its own four dimensional shape, one must keep in mind that once their existence is shaped (after death), it may be eternally unchanging and fixed. An individual's life will remain how they shaped it while living.

SIMULATION

"Life is but a dream"

When one imagines a tree, where is that tree? It is not physically in the brain, and it is not physically in reality. It is an idea perceived as an image that can be seen in the mind's eye. Physically untouchable but observable and changeable by the mind, this imagined tree is in an intangible realm of ideas and meaning. When explored further, it can be understood that the imagined tree is in the same place as a physical tree one sees, as each is an interpretation of signals and patterns in the brain that one perceives as a tree - and so both are in the mind.

Why is it that those certain signals prompt our awareness to perceive a tree, and not a wall? Why is a particular pattern in the brain interpreted as a particular thing? It suggests there may be a base code to perception where particular patterns or messages hold particular meanings and not others, and it may be inherent to consciousness and the universe.

The reality we perceive, with all the dimensions and physical laws that exist, is experienced and perceived via information only.

Signals/messages are transmitted from the senses and received and perceived by the brain. These messages are used and interpreted by the brain to construct its own model of reality, simulating what it believes the outside world to be. And so everything we sense (see, feel, smell, taste, hear) is not reality itself, but is a mental construct within the mind of what it thinks reality really is. Some refer to this as a controlled or tuned hallucination - the reality we live in our whole lives is a thought.

Like a story in a book exists in the mind of the reader, not within the actual book, the reality one experiences exists in the mind of the experiencer, not in reality itself.

The hand one sees in front of them is not their real hand, but the mind's simulated version of what their hand most likely looks like. It is all an imagined version, and may not be what the hand truly is in reality.

And colour doesn't truly exist apart from inside the mind of the observer. It is a subjective experience, not something that is real in physical reality. The sky is blue because the mind perceives certain wavelengths of light as blue, not because the sky is actually blue.

And what is true for what one sees is also true for all senses. Sound does not actually exist except for in the mind of the listener. What exists physically are only vibrations of certain frequencies within a medium. There is not a higher pitch or lower pitch, only faster and slower oscillations that the ear receives, translates into messages, and those messages are what the mind then creates the experience of sound from. And so if a tree falls and nobody is around to hear it, it doesn't make a sound, as there is no one there to experience the vibrations in the air as being sound.

In some sense, knowing that the experience one has is formed in the mind means the reality one experiences can be changed, for better or for worse, intentionally or unintentionally. A situation can depend on how you see it. Life is what you make it.

The perception of the outside can be a reflection of the inside state, as they are the same. And as thoughts can be changed, the perception of the outside can be altered or shifted. When one changes the way they look at things, the things they look at change - a dull blue can become a beautiful blue if one chooses.

The reality one sees is most likely a filtered version that is not the whole picture, but a version of reality that the mind can comprehend and understand, or a version that one is willing to accept. The human is limited in its senses, its senses are limited in their capacity for sensing, and the mind is limited in its capacity for experiencing.

And so it is that everything perceived is experienced inside the mind, and so everything perceived is the mind - everything one experiences is themselves. When one looks at a wall, they are looking at the result of their neurons firing in their brain, and so are looking at their mind's imagined version of that wall, not at the actual wall.

This means your thoughts and what you experience as physical reality are one in the same - the physical and metaphysical are one in the same. The tree one imagines and the tree one physically sees are projections of the same substance, both ideas or thoughts as real as each other. The only difference between them is one is generated by the mind and one is received by the mind. And so it begs the question, if what one sees in not reality itself, where and what is the real reality?

Interaction with reality is the brain's ability to generate new information and act in the opposite way to a receiver. Information is first received, processed, and new information is generated and sent to the mouth for speech, the hands for movement, etcetera, in order to interact with the environment.

One can not be certain whether an outside reality really exists as one sees it, or exists at all. Objective reality may be only an existence of ideas. It may be solely information and entirely mental - it may be one of primarily messages and signals both received by the mind, and generated and emanated from the mind. The brain uses these signals to construct a 'physical reality' - and while it may be experienced as physical, it is no more than a mental construct or idea based on the information received. It is a dream or thought that one doesn't realize is a dream or thought.

And if reality truly is just the communication of information, received and sent, then reality may just be a combination of all subjective realities - information received and information generated - which is shaped and changed by the collective generation and emanation of new and desired information by individuals.

If one can master generation and emanation - which is essentially imagination and action - an individual may gain abilities to manifest their desired reality. Only if coupled with undoubted belief will it be realized.

MIND'S EYE

The brain's simulation of reality can be useful knowledge when realizing our connection to the all. If we can be conscious that all is one, and everything an observer sees is themselves, then they may start to truly and consciously sense this connection in every moment.

The human form seems to separate itself from this connection to the outside world and the all. It isn't immediately apparent that instead of 'us looking at the universe', we are the universe experiencing itself, and it isn't immediately obvious that what we see when we look at the world around us is made of the same substance as what we see in our imagination.

Like a circle separating two areas on a page, only if there is a break in the circle is it open to see it is a part of the whole page. If a hole is punched through the paper, one can now see the circle as containing a hole connecting it to a higher dimensional space. It is both not separate from the 2D page it is on, and not separate from the 3D space the page resides within. This may be one way of interpreting the function of the third eye. As explained and believed by various cultures in history, the third eye is a connection to higher realities and states of being. The closing of the third eye (mind's eye) restricts access to these higher states of awareness. These higher states of awareness can be achieved when one realizes they themselves are not separate from what they see around them.

The third eye may be seen as what allows us to see the imagination, and also what receives and relays the signals from the brain to consciousness. It is second to the senses in the way that the senses relay signals to the mind, and the mind's eye is what is used to see and experience these signals as light and sound etc., essentially recreating reality within the mind in a way that allows one to understand and experience it. It is what creates an individual's simulation of reality in their mind while also being what allows the individual to view what is imagined. It is both what allows one to experience what is physical and what is not physical.

In this way the mind's eye can be seen as what allows for the view one has on what only the mind can see. This includes the subjective experience of reality one has, and the thoughts and feelings one experiences. It is what one uses to see the tree when they imagine a tree, and it is open when it is realized that this is what is used to see reality itself.

EGO

The ego is one's personality, who they believe they are, how they act and speak, their memories - it is the whole of their character that they use to interact with others and the world. It is what makes us unique and different from eachother. And since what one sees and experiences is themselves, what one sees and experiences is also the ego.

The experience one has is dictated by the ego, and determined by what lense life is looked at through and what labels the ego attaches to things. A chair is a chair because the ego has labeled it as so, otherwise it would just be an amalgamation of shapes. Likewise, a bad day is bad because the ego has labeled it as such, otherwise it is just a day.

Ego death is experiencing the absence of the ego and becoming oneself as the observer only - that point of consciousness that experiences the thoughts, emotions and everything within the experience of life.

That point of awareness is something that all individuals share and have in common. At our core, we are all the same, and it is the character we play that separates us. Our consciousness is the same, and we are our consciousness experiencing an ego. The awareness at our core is our true identity.

And while it is that when we identify with our ego we are separated, it is also what connects us. The ego allows us to interact with each other in this world, build relationships, and have an understanding of what the world is.

Many seek ego death and aim to diminish and destroy the ego, as if ego is not a good thing, however as one comes to understand what their ego truly is - which is all of their character - the importance of maintaining the ego one desires becomes apparent. An individual without an ego will amount to nothing, and will have no true way of interacting with the world.

As the ego is how an individual interacts with the world, it is how consciousness can interact with itself. The ego should be calibrated to suit one's desires. It should be treated as a friend, not an enemy.

Like anything in this existence, the ego can be both good or bad - one may have a righteous ego, one with warm intention and kind spirit. An individual may have an ego with a perspective on the world that creates a positive experience, and have an ego that actively adds value to the larger body they are a part of.

Conversely, an ego may lead one to have a negative experience. The sins mentioned in religious texts are characteristics of an ego with bad intention, and that invite negative karma (punishment). Greed, pride, lust and gluttony are all parts of an ego that are harmful to others, to themselves, and to the body of life. While these acts may provide short term pleasure for oneself, they may reflect a hedonistic lifestyle that has negative consequences for the self and/or others, and do not add overall value to life as a whole.

If one chooses to destroy their ego, they may not have control over which characteristics manifest in their ego, virtuous or sinful.

Experiencing ego death can however help an individual identify the ego, and not identify as the ego, which helps to identify their true self as awareness. It may also allow an individual rebuild the ego in the way they desire.

Working with one's ego and encouraging good behaviors and actions in oneself is important to gaining control over and living a fulfilling life. The ego is a friend, not an enemy, and should be treated as such.

Self talk is an effective tool for aiding with this control. If one self criticizes or self doubts, and their self talk is negative, it is self limiting. Complaining is one behavior that forces negative focus. A more positive tone can be created in the mind with conscious effort and constant identification and adjustment of the self talk one is engaging in.

Perceived negative experiences can become constructive lessons if one chooses to look at them this way - it is not what happens, it's what you do. Understanding one's ego can set the direction and experience of one's life to a more desired state, and should not ever be underestimated.

MANIFESTATION

"Life is what you make it"

In modern culture, manifestation is the ideology that with true belief that an outcome will be realized, it will be.

In a physicalist sense, if one knows where they would like to be in life, opportunities that present themselves to a person then hold a value as to whether or not it will help them to reach the desired outcome, and so it is much easier to follow the correct path towards it. One must however first fully believe the outcome is possible for this to work.

As previously stated, if existence is solely information, then generation and emanation of new and desired information may allow one to manifest their desired reality. It may be that the belief behind this information determines how real it becomes. Manifestation is also sometimes described as a calling for higher beings, such as life itself or the all, to aid in guiding one toward a desired outcome, which resembles prayer more than what manifestation is usually defined as. Regardless of the method used or the interpretation of its workings, a level of belief is required.
Belief is a tool used by most if not all religions, medicine and is described in various practices of modern spirituality. Whether it is belief in future outcomes, one's self, or a higher power, faith and belief have real world uses and benefits.

Science is impressed and thoroughly in support of the effectiveness of the placebo effect, an effect reliant on belief. If a patient truly believes there will be benefit in a medication, then there likely will be, even if the medication is actually non-existent. This does not discount or nullify outcomes that are a result of the placebo effect, but rather should demonstrate the realness of the effect itself and the power belief holds. The placebo effect is a term commonly used to discount outcomes (for example, *'it's just a placebo, it doesn't actually work'*), however, it does actually work, and it should not be seen this way. Placebo is just one name for a phenomena whereby belief causes a desired outcome. The effect is as powerful and the outcomes are as real as any other.

In religion, prayer can be seen as another method where belief is used to manifest an outcome. True belief that prayer will help reach a desired outcome allows for the outcome to be realized. Unlike hope, it must be wholly true and undoubted belief - a belief so strong that one could describe it as knowing.

Prayer is described differently to manifestation as it has the intention of conversing with a higher being to help reach a desired outcome, while manifestation usually puts emphasis on the individual manifesting as the cause of the outcome. Prayer and manifestation have more in common than not - both require belief that an outcome will be realized via an unseeable force.

While it takes a level of faith for these methods to work, they do work. An individual's future can be shaped by the individual, and the only limit to outcomes is belief.

Because the evidence of these effects can only be experienced subjectively and relayed anecdotally, one must experience it for themselves to fully understand its power. Experience is the evidence.

Countless analogous methods have been described as or in the name of witchcraft, voodoo, contemporary spirituality, and religion, and includes manifestation, prayer, placebo, good luck charms, magic, and many others. All of these involve doing anything with the belief it will achieve a desired outcome.

And so, reaching a desired outcome may simply be influenced by one's free will to have belief.

As the universe is imagined, and imagined items and perceived items are made of the same substance, one can influence and shape the perceived as much as the imagined.

With infinite potential outcomes possible, and infinite potential outcomes imaginable, our ability to imagine an outcome does not make the outcome real, but makes it potential - and so imagination in this sense can be seen as an ability to perceive potentialities. This coupled with belief and action can act like a rudder, guiding ones fall through time and potentialities toward a desired destination.

Often it is only the destination that needs to be known, and the path will build itself. Worrying about or trying to control how one will reach a destination only limits the paths that can be taken to get there.

One must know their destination will be reached, but will not know when the door to it will open. When that door does open, walk through.

If one can visualize a desired future outcome, and has undoubted belief this will be realized, then it will be, as long as the presented opportunities to get there are taken.

MENTAL TRANSMUTATION

"If you change the way you look at things, the things you look at change"

If you expect a situation or day to not be good, it likely will not be good. The brain's focus on negatives will overrule any positives experienced when looking through a negative lense, and vice versa.

It can take mental effort to change one's outlook, and a resignation of the ego's attachment to reasoning for why something won't be good, however if one can do this, a bad situation can drastically change for the better.

MENTAL ASSOCIATION

Mental association is the act of associating two or more mental items for various reasons, including but not limited to enhancing memory, stimulating a physiological response, and achieving a desired mental state.

Once one understands that the mind functions off associations, it opens the doors to almost unlimited applications. The mind associates sounds with words, words with meaning, faces with names, places with emotions, emotions with memories. Everything the mind seems to do is underpinned with associating one thing with another.

One example that demonstrates the fundamentals of association is pavlov's dogs, whereby a bell is sounded every time a dog is given food. The food stimulates an unconscious prompt for the dog to salivate, and after enough repetition of this, association allows for the bell alone to become a stimulus for salivation, even in the absence of food.

This principle can be applied to any mind, for any purpose, and its power cannot be overstated.

One application of this is hand positioning, often used by people in power and the occult. This is used to induce a mental state, where each hand sign has already been associated with a state of being. When one is in a powerful state of mind or situation, particular hand positioning can be used to associate this state of being with this particular hand sign. Once set, this can then be used in reverse. When one wants to feel powerful, they are able to use the hand sign they associated with feeling powerful to induce that feeling again.

This is much like how breathing is already associated with states of being. When in a calm state, slow and steady breathing is automatic. This can be utilized in reverse, where if one wishes to feel calm, a slow and steady breath can be practiced to induce this state.

Understanding both the potential of creating associations and of utilizing already existing associations can allow for some power to control one's own mind.

MENTAL ASSOCIATION FOR CONDITIONING

A common use of association is exposure therapy, whereby gradually exposing oneself to fears and anxieties in a safe environment can re-associate these conditions with not fear but comfortability. This can aid in overcoming feelings about certain situations and recondition the mind.

This can also be used in conjunction with the mental association of breath. Instigating a fast and deep breath pattern similar to that of a panicking individual will induce a stress response, release adrenaline and cause a state of alertness. If one practices this breath pattern and exposes themselves to this stress state while maintaining a mental state of calmness, a relaxed body, and meditating into the moment, they can condition themselves to be in control if a real state of stress is ever experienced.

This has famously been popularized by wim hof, whereby 30 breaths of near hyperventilation is undertaken, followed by breathing out and holding the out breath for one to three minutes. This is just one method of exposure therapy and mental association to help cope with stress.

Similarly, the practice of meditation is done to strengthen the ability of bringing the mind's attention back to the moment and reduce unwanted thoughts. While sitting quietly, the mind wanders, and when it is noticed that it has wandered, simply bring it back to the moment by noticing the breath. When practiced, this ability is strengthened like a muscle, and the wandering mind and racing thoughts become more easily managed over time.

And while through practices can the mind be managed, so can it be managed through thought and understanding. For example, one can understand that when in a good state of mind, certain things won't bother a person; an unpleasant encounter won't feel worth worrying over. When in a bad state of mind, these things may be a bother and add to negative mood, however understanding that there is a state of mind in which the particular thing doesn't matter as much shows the reality of the thing itself. Why should it matter now if it doesn't matter while in a different mood? Why let it get to you now that you're feeling vulnerable, when the truth as seen from another perspective is that it doesn't matter at all.

There are many ways to manage the mind, and through practice it may be mastered.

MENTAL ASSOCIATION FOR MEMORY

Mental association can also be utilized for memory. This is commonly achieved through use of mnemonics. A simple introduction into mnemonics is the example of remembering a list of items.

Given a list of many random and unrelated items, such as a shopping list, it may seem absolutely necessary to write the list down in order to remember it fully and correctly, however a simple mnemonic technique can allow for an accurate and complete unaided recall of each item. This involves associating each word with the next in a story format visualized in the mind.

For example, in the case of remembering the following list:

1. Hand
2. Leaf
3. Fish
4. Planet
5. Dirt

One can visualize a hand, and the hand is fragile and made of leaves. A fish bites one of the leaf fingers off, and then the fish inflates rapidly to become planet sized. The fish planet then ages and erodes into dirt.

The more absurd and emotionally stimulating the story, the easier the recall of the words are. These stories can be made up and visualized with ease, and the effect it has on one's ability to recall items in order is drastic.

A more advanced mnemonic used to remember items like these is called the mental palace. This is where items are associated with the mental imagery of walking through a familiar house or building in one's mind.

For the list above, this may be done by visualizing walking up the driveway of your childhood home in your mind, and imagining the driveway is made out of hands grabbing at your feet. When you reach the door, the door is made of leaves, its texture and appearance vividly imagined. When the door handle is reached for, it is noticed that the handle is made from a live, slimy fish. Once the door is opened, there is a void of space inside, with a single floating planet in the center made from dirt.

These techniques can be continued for any number of items, and it can be surprising how effortless the recall of items can be when using them.

Finally, a common mnemonic for remembering numbers of any length (for example pi, or a phone number) is by assigning and associating each number with a certain item. An easy way of remembering these items is using words that rhyme with each number, for example:

Zero - hero
One - bun
Two - shoe
Three - tree
Four - door
Five - hive
Six - sticks
Seven - heaven
Eight - gate
Nine - line

These can then be arranged in a story like format to quickly remember any number one wants to remember, of any length. Again, the more engaging and absurd the story is, the easier it is for the mind to remember it.

For the first five digits of pi, 3.1415, one might imagine a tree (3) with bread buns (1) as its fruit. A door (4) opens in the trunk of the tree to reveal it is filled with these bread buns (1), however a single beehive (5) is among the bread buns, oozing honey all over them.

While these techniques require a strong imagination, the mind remembers stories with far more ease than raw data, and so they work with surprising accuracy and effectiveness.

RELIGION AND SCIENCE

"It is said one needs to see to believe, but sometimes one must believe to see"

Many argue whether it is religion or science that holds truth, however they are not mutually exclusive - it is science and religion, not science or religion. While science holds value for the physical, religion and spirituality hold value for the metaphysical - that which is not physical, such as thoughts, feelings and consciousness. The existence of the non-physical cannot be proven, yet its existence is subjectively obvious.

Religious texts such as the bible and the quran are writings and teachings based on the laws of the universe - not physical laws, but those of the human experience. Some refer to these laws as moral laws, however they extend beyond morals.

Individuals may say they can have a moral compass without religion, but one must ask where do they find these morals for themselves? They don't create what is right or wrong, but can feel and sense them to be so. It is not an external teaching that dictates what is right and wrong, but something intrinsic. They inherently exist in the immaterial metaphysical realm. These rules are written into the universe, and these are accessible to all.

It is not just those of religion that know that laziness (sloth), pride and exultance, murder and intentional harm, adultery, and the many sins in religious texts can lead to a worse overall human experience and suffering. It is not just those of religion that know that kindness is rewarded with a good feeling for oneself and others. These are universal laws, written into the nature of the universe. Most individuals, regardless of religious affiliation, know these as facts and as obvious, and that these always will be true.

It is when these rules have been explored and noted onto paper do we receive some of "God's word" in religious texts.

The texts also make reference to common experiences such as mental health disorders like depression and anxiety represented by and corresponding to demons or negative entities. They also reference common structures that appear in reality such as hierarchy and the dimensional layers of the universe. These texts take note of what seems to be universal in reality, as presented by reality itself.

These universal laws are similar to mathematical truths in the way that they do not exist in the physical but are still as real as the physical. Mathematics are concepts, ideas and rules that are immaterial in themselves, even if they describe the material world. They are perceptual ideas that are independent of one's own perception. And so they exist without an observer, but do not exist in physicality. So where do they exist? These ideas are metaphysical, and exist in the mind of the universe.

Discerning which religion is the truth can be challenging to approach.

A common atheist argument is to question the chances that one's chosen religion is the correct one - they conclude that a believer of one discipline is essentially an atheist to all other religions. Many religions hold themselves as separate, however many seem to be analogous, describe the same ideas, and promote positivity, compassion and kindness, and so should not be so divisive in their disciplines and so particular in their defense of details.

The different religions are like a father teaching his children the same lessons and knowledge in different ways to suit each child's unique needs. Because the lessons are taught differently does not mean that one is more correct. They all lead to the same place.

If a father tells his children to write a story about the same thing, each child's story will be slightly different. It does not mean the stories do not contain the same message.

In this way, religions seem to pertain to the same ideas - they consist of the written rules of the mental universe. Each religion teaches of these same teachings, and describe the same dichotomies of good and evil, yin and yang, God and devil. Each are different paths that aim toward to same thing. The rules and lessons are similar or the same across cultures, as they are sourced from the same place. They are written into the metaphysical universe and the experience of life - good is good, bad is bad, and the causes of each are consistent.

Most religious texts aim to use these observations of these laws of the universe to encourage and help individuals navigate a good experience, however some may have been wrongly used to perpetuate suffering and encourage inequality.

These texts can be important tools to help individuals navigate life and these laws for themselves, and may be used to aid in ones understanding of how a more positive way of living can be achieved.

4

FRACTAL FORCES

&
RELEVANT FEATURES

GRAVITY

The inward force of gravity and the perceived inward direction of higher dimensions is a relationship explained by a simple analogy.

A ball of a certain mass is placed in the center of a tightly suspended elastic sheet.

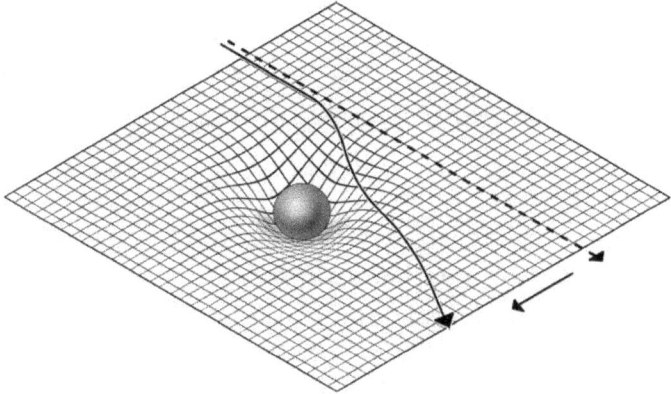

In the analogy, we can interpret the sheet as being a 2D fabric of existence, and the ball being an object with a mass within that existence. The fabric can be seen to be distorted and pulled, not in any direction within the 2D existence, but it gets pulled and distorted into the third dimension.

When a second object is placed on the 2D sheet, the objects seem to attract each other, and with their mass combined they both can reach a further distance in the third dimension, increasing the distortion of space, and increasing the perceived force of gravity.

In this way, gravity seems to be a distortion of the fabric of space-time into the dimension above it, perceived by humans as an inward force that acts toward higher dimensions - just as it was explored in an earlier section that distance in higher dimensions is perceived as inwards (inwards is upwards). This applies to the third and fourth dimensions, and fourth and fifth. The experience of gravity is the experience of falling toward higher dimensions.

The perceived strength or force of gravity an object has is directly related to the distance it distorts the fabric of its dimensional plane into the dimension above. The larger the mass, the larger the distortion, and the larger the force perceived.

The above analogy for gravity can be applied to any number of dimensions, and may be even more plainly understood by simplifying it to the first and second dimensions:

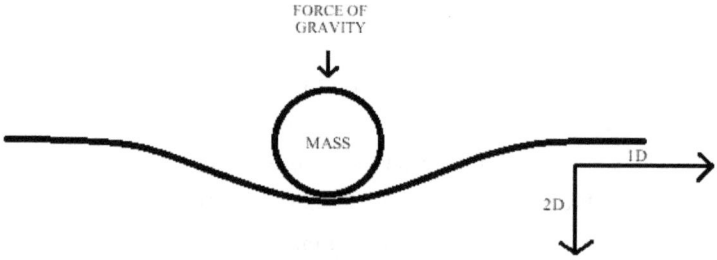

Where a mass is distorting the one dimensional fabric of this hypothetical existence into the second dimension.

The analogy for gravity when applied to higher dimensions can be used to explain the pace at which time moves for an observer.

While from chapter one it can be understood that the dimensional perspective of an observer is responsible for the direction that time is perceived, gravity (dimensional distortion) is responsible for the pace that an observer perceives time. The stronger the force of gravity an individual experiences, the slower that individual ages compared to an individual experiencing less gravity. This is famously outlined by einstein in his theory of general relativity, which can be useful to look into if one wishes to understand this further. Essentially, the distance an individual is in higher dimensions corresponds to how fast one falls or is 'pulled' forward in time.

And so the pace of time perceived is a result of the magnitude of distortion of one dimension into another, the direction of time perceived is a result of an individual's dimensional perspective in the universe, and lateral movement in time (towards differing outcomes) is allowed by the universe being comprised of at least 5 dimensions.

THE EXPANDING UNIVERSE

The universe is expanding, and as this expansion is observed, scientists conclude through what is called red shift that the objects further away from us in the universe seem to be traveling away from us faster than those closer to us.

Red shift is the process whereby the light waves from something traveling away from an observer will be stretched, and so the frequency of those light waves will decrease. This in turn will make the light coming off that object shift down in the light spectrum towards red. The faster an object is traveling away from an observer, the more that red shift will occur, and the more red the object will appear.

More distant objects in the universe appear to have more red shift than those closer to us, and so we can infer that they are traveling away from us faster.

The reason that objects further away from us in the universe appear to be traveling away from us faster can be explained using a dimensional analogy.

If the universe is represented as the 2D surface of an inflating balloon, the center of the inflating balloon is where the universe is expanding from. If planets and stars can be represented as dots or points on the surface of the inflating balloon, it would appear that these dots are expanding away from each other. If an observer is represented as one dot on the surface of the balloon, it would appear that planets and stars further away from that observer are expanding away faster than those closer to the observer. This also gives the illusion that each planet or star seems to be the center point of where the universe is expanding from, however the expansion is actually occurring from a higher dimensional location, which is the center of the 3D balloon, not from any point on the 2D surface.

When using this analogy for higher dimensions, we can apply this expansion to time. If the passage of time is represented as the circumference of an expanding circle, the center of that circle is where time is expanding from, not anywhere on the circumference. And so the universe may not have a start in the way we would imagine it to. The center of the expanding circle is the start of the universe, not forwards or backwards in time as humans perceive it. The amount of time in the universe increases, but it does not have a beginning that is easy for us to imagine. It is like the balloon inflating and we are on the surface. It expands in all areas visible to us at the same time, but we cannot see where it is truly inflating from, as that is in a higher dimensional area than we are.

THE SHAPE OF THE UNIVERSE

Following from the analogy of the relationships dimensions have to each other, the conceptualizations and relationships between the dimensions can be applied to shapes other than a square → cube → hypercube, but with some differences for a circle.

A square consists of four 1D lines defining its bound, and contains infinite 1D lines within it.

A triangle consists of three 1D lines defining its bound, and contains infinite 1D lines within it.

A circle consists of zero 1D lines defining its bound, but instead consists of infinite 0D points defining its bound, and contains infinite 1D lines within it.

A sphere consists of infinite 0D points defining its bound, and contains infinite 2D circles within it.

A hypersphere consists of infinite 0D points defining its bound, and contains infinite 3D spheres within it.

This may first be thought to manifest as the seemingly infinite spheres (planets and stars) we observe, however this ultimately allows for any point to be the apparent center of the universe, rather than a finite number of potential centers if it were to be any other higher dimensional shape.

While the shape of the universe being a higher dimensional sphere isn't truly known, we know that it is a higher than three dimensional shape, and the implications of this are important.

If an ant travels in a straight line around a two dimensional circle, it will reach where it started. If a human were to travel in a straight line around the three dimensional sphere of earth, they will eventually arrive at where they started.

Following this analogy, if an observer travels in a straight line through a four dimensional hypersphere (space-time), they will eventually arrive again to where they began. This is true for space *and* time, as an observer traveling forward in time to the 'end' will reach the beginning of time again. If one were to travel through the seemingly boundless area of space in a straight line, they will eventually arrive back to where they started.

There is no true beginning to the universe or time in the way we would like to imagine it. Like a pole on a sphere, if you keep traveling towards it you will end up traveling away from it again. If you continue traveling south you end up traveling north. If you continue back in time, you will end up traveling forward in time. There is no true edge to this universe, as there is no edge of earth - there is no beginning or end. However if traveling along the circumference of a circle represented traveling through time, the start would be the center of the circle.

6

REVELATION

TO LIVE LIFE

"The journey leads back to the beginning"

While the search for the meaning and structure of the universe can be fulfilling, at the end of it some realize the magic in it is the not knowing. There is a sense of wonder and magic in the fact that things just are, and not knowing how or why.

Like a movie director who has crafted a movie, they can now see behind the curtains and notice the mistakes within the film. They notice the actors are just acting, and aren't actually the characters portrayed. They understand how the special effects were created. They know the ending and each scene that is to come. And so this can make it difficult to immerse themselves in the film like a normal viewer would.

Much the same, part of what gives life its magic is its mystery. Sometimes it is better to live and enjoy than to worry about the why, what and how of it. Let go and enjoy the journey while you are here, taking each step as it comes.

www.ingramcontent.com/pod-product-compliance
Lightning Source LLC
Chambersburg PA
CBHW070800050426
42452CB00012B/2418